リック式「右脳」メソッド

ヤバいくらい使える

「起きてから寝るまで」

英会話

リック西尾

リーディング

1回読み通すごとにワンチェック

1	2	3	4
9	10	11	12
17	18	19	20
25	26	27	28
33	34	35	36

チェックシート

40回リーディングできたら完璧!!

5	6	7	8
13	14	15	16
21	22	23	24
29	30	31	32
37	38	39	40

はじめに

　こんな話があります。ある人が日本に来て間もない中国人に聞いたそうです。
「あなたは日本語がお上手ですね」
「以前から勉強されていたのですか？」
「いいえ日本に来てから勉強しました」
「でもどうしてそんなに上手に話せるのですか？」
「あたりまえでしょ。もう4ヶ月も勉強しているんですよ」
「！？……」
　その人は返す言葉がなかったそうです。
　私たち日本人は中学・高校と、少なくとも6年間英語を勉強してきました。しかしそれなのに、大半の人がカタコトの英語すら話すことができません。そして英語アレルギーになっています。ですから日本に来て間もない外国人が、スラスラと日本語を話すのを目の当たりにすると、驚いてしまうのです。
　当然その中国人は、充分に日本語を話すことはできないはずです。でも6年間も英語を勉強しても会話ができない私たちにしてみれば驚きです。外国語を勉強すれば話すことができるのは当然と考える外国人と、簡単な挨拶すら英語でできない日本人。いったい何が違うのでしょうか。

ここで皆さんに質問です。以下の文を英語で言えますか。

「風邪をひいたみたいです」

「咳が止まりません」

「鼻水が出ます」

「下痢が続いています」

「食欲がありません」

「便秘が続いています」

　日本語なら小学生でも言える内容です。しかしそれが英語となると大半の方は言えません。難解な英単語を知っているのに、何と英語で表現すればいいかわかりません。それはなぜでしょうか。実は私たちは中学・高校・大学受験の過程で、上記の英語表現を習ってこなかったのです。**習わなければ話せるはずがありません。**

　日本における学校の英語教育は、足早にレベルが上がっていきます。大学受験になると難しい英単語を詰め込み、難解な英文解釈を求められます。6年間でできるだけ高いレベルまで英語を習得させようとする方針のために、実際に使える英語の習得を犠牲にしてしまっているのです。ですから「鼻水が出ます」ということすら英語で言えないのです。もし仮に6年間、実際のコミュニケーションで使える英語を中心とした授業を学校で行っていれば、これほど多くの日本人が英語が話せないという結果にはならなかったことでしょう。

先ほどの中国人が、いとも容易に日本語を習得することができたその秘訣は、日本語を話せるようになることをまず第1の目標として勉強したからです。

　ですから英語をマスターするためには、難解な英文解釈を学習するより、まず話せることを目標に英語を学習したほうがいいのです。

　外国語を勉強する時に大切なのは、まず自分に身近な関心のあることから学ぶのが秘訣です。自分に関係がなく関心のないことは、たとえ一生懸命に覚えてもすぐに忘れてしまい身につきません。でも関心のあることなら容易に覚えることができますし、習得することができます。

　本書は起きてから寝るまでに交わす会話を、英語で表現することができるようにすることが目的です。よくある日常のワンシーンを区切って、当たり前に交わすであろう日常会話の表現を集めました。

　登場人物の会話の中には、以外と知られていない口語表現が織り込まれています。あなたが英語を身につける上できっと役に立つと思います。

　ところで語学を習得するうえで大切なことは、反復練習です。スポーツでも、楽器の演奏でも、ダンスでも、それをマスターするためには実際にカラダを動かして何度も同じことを反復するトレーニングが不可欠です。従来の学校での英語教育で欠落していたのが、口を動かし

て何度も反復することだったのです。

　ですから読者の皆さんは、本書を1回読んだだけで終わりにしないで欲しいのです。本がボロボロになるまで声に出して読み返し、英語が自然と口について出るようになるまで反復トレーニングをして欲しいのです。

　学習の手順としては、まず全文を読み英語の意味を理解してください。日本文と英文が合致しない文章が多少ありますが、これは日本人とアメリカ人の発想の違いによるものです。その点をご理解ください。

　次に英語の音声データをダウンロードし、何度も音声をヒアリングして耳を慣らしてください。また音声を真似して、同じように発音できるまでスピーキングを繰り返してください。

　最後に左ページの日本語を英語で表現できるまで反復し内容を覚えてください。

　巻頭にチェックチャートを用意しています。40回を目安にチャートにチェックしながら学習を進めてください。40回が終わった頃には、自然と英語が口について話せるようになっていることを実感することでしょう。

　本書が皆さんの英語習得の一助となれば幸いです。

リック西尾

```
すべての英文の音声入り
無料音声
（1～4倍速対応）
ダウンロード
スマホでも聴けます！
```

本書の英文の音声は、パソコン・スマホ・タブレット端末のいずれでも無料でご利用いただけます。ダウンロードの詳細は、下記をご参照ください。

http://kklong.co.jp/okitekara

下のQRコードからもアクセスできます。

■2倍速、3倍速、4倍速でチャレンジしてみよう！

　最初は通常のスピードで英文を聞き、声に出して下さい。少し慣れてきたら2倍速でチャレンジして下さい。それにも慣れてきたら3倍速に、さらに4倍速にまでチャレンジして下さい。

　やっているうちに左脳の自意識が薄れ、情報が右脳に定着しやすくなります。右脳に定着した英語の情報が左脳につながれば、いつでも理解し表現ができるようになります。そして自然に英語が口から出てくるようになります。

　このチャレンジの過程で、日本語という振動数の低い言語に慣れ切っていた聴覚が鋭くなってくるのが分かります。聴覚が敏感になることによって、振動数の高い英文を聞き取る力が高まります。

　試しに、高速に慣れてきたら、少しスピードを下げてみてください。以前は聞きにくかった英文がハッキリ聞こえ、いつの間にか右脳に定着しているのが実感できるはずです。

〈指導・制作〉
一般社団法人エジソン・アインシュタインスクール協会

代表　鈴木昭平

リーディングチェックシート
はじめに

第1章

今日は日本語禁止の日、朝から英語で大騒ぎ 17

起床① Getting Up 1

起床② Getting Up 2

起床③ Getting Up 3

起床④ Getting Up 4

病気① Illness 1

病気② Illness 2

朝のひととき In the Morning

朝食 Breakfast

出勤① Going to Work 1

出勤② Going to Work 2

出勤③ Going to Work 3

洗濯・掃除 Doing Laundry and Cleaning

赤ちゃんの世話 Taking Care of a Baby

ペットの世話 Taking Care of a Pet

会社① At Work 1

会社② At Work 2

会社③	At Work 3
会社④	At Work 4
会社⑤	At Work 5
会社⑥	At Work 6
会社⑦	At Work 7

第2章

お昼過ぎ、電話も あいさつも英語で　61

電話①	Telephone 1
電話②	Telephone 2
電話③	Telephone 3
電話④	Telephone 4
電話⑤	Telephone 5
電話⑥	Telephone 6
電話⑦	Telephone 7
電話⑧	Telephone 8
あいさつ①	Saying Hello 1
あいさつ②	Saying Hello 2
久しぶりの再会①	Reunion 1
久しぶりの再会②	Reunion 2
久しぶりの再会③	Reunion 3

別れのあいさつ①　Saying Goodbye 1

別れのあいさつ②　Saying Goodbye 2

第3章

午後のひととき、まだ英語でいける！

93

天気のあいさつ①　Talking about the Weather 1

天気のあいさつ②　Talking about the Weather 2

天気のあいさつ③　Talking about the Weather 3

天気のあいさつ④　Talking about the Weather 4

日時をたずねる①　Asking the Time and Date 1

日時をたずねる②　Asking the Time and Date 2

駅で①　At the Station 1

駅で②　At the Station 2

バス停で　At the Bus Stop

タクシー①　Taxi 1

タクシー②　Taxi 2

道をたずねる①　Asking Directions 1

道をたずねる②　Asking Directions 2

道をたずねる③　Asking Directions 3

第4章

外出中も
英語ですごそう　123

訪問①　Visiting 1
訪問②　Visiting 2
紹介　Introductions
写真　Taking Pictures
おいとま　Heading Home
ファーストフード　Fast Food
ショッピング①　Shopping 1
ショッピング②　Shopping 2
ショッピング③　Shopping 3
ショッピング④　Shopping 4
ショッピング⑤　Shopping 5
ショッピング⑥　Shopping 6
ショッピング⑦　Shopping 7
美容室①　Beauty Shop 1
美容室②　Beauty Shop 2
歯科医院　Dentist
病院①　At the Doctor 1
病院②　At the Doctor 2
病院③　At the Doctor 3

病院④　At the Doctor 4

ドライブ　Going for a Drive

自動車事故　Car Accident

犯罪①　Crime 1

犯罪②　Crime 2

第5章

そろそろ日も沈むころ、英語だけですごせた？ 173

頼みごと　Asking a Favor

デートに誘う①　Asking Someone for a Date 1

デートに誘う②　Asking Someone for a Date 2

デートに誘う③　Asking Someone for a Date 3

アフター6　After Work

夕方　Evening

夕食①　Dinner 1

夕食②　Dinner 2

お出かけ　Going Out

レストラン①　Restaurant 1

レストラン②　Restaurant 2

レストラン③　Restaurant 3

レストラン④　Restaurant 4

レストラン⑤　Restaurant 5

レストラン⑥　Restaurant 6

レストラン⑦　Restaurant 7

支払い　Payment

映画　Movie

カラオケ　Karaoke

愛の告白　Confessing Love to Someone

テレビ　TV

飲み屋①　Bar 1

飲み屋②　Bar 2

飲み屋③　Bar 3

夜のひととき　At Night

就寝　Going to Bed

第1章

今日は日本語禁止の日、朝から英語で大騒ぎ

起床①

あなた、もう朝ですよ

起きる時間ですよ

早く起きないと会社に遅れるわよ

うるさいな〜

もうちょっと寝かせてくれよ

知らないわよ、会社に遅刻しても

わかってる

もう起こさないからね

いつまでも寝ていたら…

英語表現

① honey　おまえ、あなた（妻・夫・恋人・子供に対する呼びかけ）
② annoying　彫 うるさくする
③ Let A do　A を…させよ
④ blame　をとがめる

Getting Up 1

Honey, it's morning already.
①

Time to get up.

You'll be late for work if you don't get up now.

How annoying...
　　アノイイング
②

Let me sleep just a few more minutes.
③

Don't blame me if you're late for work.
　　　　ブレイム
④

I know.

I'm not going to wake you up anymore.
　　　⑤　　　　　　　⑥

Stay in bed as long as you want...
　　　　　　　⑦

⑤not...anymore　もう2度と…しない
⑥wake(up)　を起こす
⑦as long as...　…の間は

19

起床②

ねえ、一郎、もう7時だよ

起きてる？

ああ…

よく眠れた？

まだ眠いよ

なんだか寝不足みたいだな

いやな夢を見てしまったよ

君のいびきがひどかったし

あれじゃ眠れやしないよ

英語表現
① sleepy　形 眠い
② have a dream　夢を見る
③ snore　いびきをかく
④ heavily　副 激しく

Getting Up 2

Hey, Ichiro, it's already 7.

Are you up?

Yeah...

Did you sleep well?

I'm still sleepy.
①

I don't think I had enough sleep.

I had a bad dream.
②

And you were snoring heavily, too.
スノー(ア)イング
③ ④

No wonder I can't get a good night's rest.
⑤

⑤ No wonder...　…は不思議ではない

21

起床③

あなた、もうとっくに 7 時過ぎてるわよ

いま何時だ?

7 時半よ

何、7 時半!?

どうして起こしてくれなかったんだ?

寝過ごしてしまったじゃないか

さっきから起こしてるじゃない

ああっ、完全に遅刻だ!

お前のせいだぞ!

英語表現

① way　副 随分
② oversleep　寝過ごす
③ some time　しばらく
④ (Good, My, Oh) God!　しまった、大変だ!

Getting Up 3

Honey, it's way past 7:00.
①

What time is it now?

It's 7:30.

What? 7:30!?

Why didn't you wake me up?

I overslept.
②

I've been trying to wake you up for some time.
③

God, I'm totally late!
④ ⑤

It's your fault!
⑥
フォールト

⑤ late 形 遅刻した
⑥ fault （過失の）責任

23

起床④

久美子、おはよう

あなたようやく起きたのね

どうしたの？

元気ないわね

具合でも悪いの？

二日酔いらしい

頭がガンガンする

だからあれほど言ったじゃない

飲み過ぎないようにって

英語表現

① awake 囲 目が覚めて
② look A （外観が）A に見える
③ hangover 二日酔い
④ have got を持っている

Getting Up 4

Good morning, Kumiko.

Finally, you're <u>awake</u>.
  　　　　　　 ①

What's wrong?

You don't <u>look</u> good.
  　　　　　②

Are you feeling bad?

　　　　　　　　　　 ハングオウヴァ
I seem to have a <u>hangover</u>.
  　　　　　　　　　　 ③

　　　　　　バウンディング
I've got a <u>pounding</u> headache.
  ④　　　　　 ⑤

<u>That's why</u> I told you
  ⑥

not to drink too much.

⑤ pound　ドンドンたたく
⑥ That's why　そういうわけで…なのです

25

病気①

ねえ、あなた顔色悪いわよ

具合が悪いの？

んん、ちょっとな

体調がよくないの？

カラダがだるいんだ

手もしびれるし

それは困ったわね

今日会社休んで

医者に行ってきたらどう？

英語表現

① pale　形 青白い
② feel A　Aと感じる
③ a little bit　ちょっと
④ numb　形 しびれた

Illness 1

Hey, look at your face, it's so pale.
①
ペイル

Are you feeling bad?
②

Umm, a little bit.
③

Are you sick?

My body feels heavy.

My hands are numb, too.
④
ナ　ム

That's not good.

Why don't you take a day off today
⑤

and go see a doctor?
⑥

⑤ take a day off　1日休暇をとる
⑥ see a doctor　医者に診てもらう

27

病気②

ハクション！

あらどうしたの、くしゃみなんかして？

どうやら風邪ひいちゃったみたいだ

喉が痛いし

寒気がする

体温計で熱を測ってみて

あらいやだ、39度もあるわよ

ひどい熱じゃない

そんなに熱があるのか？

英語表現
① sneeze　くしゃみをする
② seem like...　…のように思われる
③ hurt　痛む
④ temperature　体温

Illness 2

アチュー
Achoo!

スニージング
What's wrong, sneezing like that?
        ①

Seems like I have a cold.
 ②

スロウト ハ～ツ
My throat hurts, and
       ③

I feel a chill.

テンペラチ(ュ)ア   サ マ メ タ ァ
Take your temperature with the thermometer.
         ④   ⑤

ディグリーズ
Oh my God, it's 39 degrees.
               ⑥

It's so bad.

Do I have that much of a temperature?

⑤ thermometer　体温計
⑥ degree　度

朝のひととき

いったい誰だよ、トイレに入っているのは？

いつまで中に入ってるんだ？

5分以上経ってるぞ

早く出てくれ！

漏れそうだよ！

なんだ、おまえか

朝は忙しいんだ

早く用を足せよ

パパ、トイレットペーパーもうないよ

英語表現

① in the world　一体全体（疑問文を強める）
② like　副 おそらく
③ Come on out！　さあ、出てくれ！
④ wet　をぬらす

In the Morning

Who in the world is in the bathroom?
①

How long do you think you've been in there?

It's like more than 5 minutes.
②

Hurry. Come on out!
③

I'm going to wet my pants!
④

Oh, it was you.
⑤

People are busy in the morning.

Hurry up.
⑥

Dad, there's no toilet paper.

⑤ oh　おや、まあ（驚き）
⑥ hurry up　急ぐ（主に命令文で用いる）

31

朝食

ねえ、あなた、朝食はどうする？

食べてる時間なんかないよ

そんなこと言わないで、食べてったら

体によくないわよ

わかった、食べてくよ

コーヒーとミルクどっちにする？

ミルクちょうだい

ゴクゴクゴク

さあ、出かけるとするか…

英語表現

① sweetie（=darling） ねえ、あなた
② What about...? …はいかがですか？
③ would like A A が欲しいのですが
④ gulp ゴクリと飲む

Breakfast

Hey sweetie, what about breakfast?
<u>①</u>　　　<u>②</u>

I don't have time for breakfast.

Don't say like that. You should eat something.

It's not good for your health.

All right. I'll eat something.

Would you like coffee or milk?
<u>③</u>

Give me some milk.

Gulp, gulp, gulp.
<u>④</u>

Well, I'll get going then...
<u>⑤</u>　　　<u>⑥</u>　　　<u>⑦</u>

⑤ well　さて、ええと
⑥ get doing　…し始める
⑦ then　副 それでは

33

出勤①

今日はどの洋服で行こうかしら？

これは昨日着てったし…

これでいいか

あらいやだ、この服カビがはえてる

お気に入りの服なのに…

クリーニングに出さなくちゃ

あら、もう時間だわ

あれ、ハンドバックがない

どこに置いたっけ…？

英語表現

① Oh dear!　まあ、どうしましょう！
② moldy　㊟ かびがはえている
③ favorite　㊟ 気に入っている
④ have got to do　…しなければならない

34

Going to Work 1

What clothes should I wear for work today?

I wore this yesterday...

Maybe this one.

Oh dear, it's moldy.
① ②

フェイヴ(ァ)リト
My favorite dress...
③

I've got to take it to the dry cleaners.
④ ⑤

My goodness! Time to go.
⑥

Oh no! My handbag's missing.
⑦

Where did I leave it...?

⑤ the dry cleaners　ドライクリーニング店
⑥ (Oh,) my goodness!　なんということだ！
⑦ missing　形 行方不明の

35

出勤②

ああっ、もうこんな時間だ！

遅れているぞ

このままだと会社に遅刻してしまう

急がなくては

良かった

ぎりぎり間に合った

あれ、定期券がない？

しまった、置き忘れてきてしまった

おれはいったい何を考えているんだ？

英語表現

① gee　おやおや
② run　（事が）継続する
③ the way things stand now　このままでは
④ had better do　…したほうがよい

Going to Work 2

Gee, look at the time!
①

I'm running late.
②

I'll be late for work the way things stand now.
③

I'd better hurry.
④

Lucky me.
⑤

I just made it.
⑥

Where's my commuter pass?
コミューター

Shoot. I forgot it.
⑦

What am I thinking of?
⑧

⑤ Lucky me.　ついている
⑥ make it　うまくいく
⑦ shoot　ちえっ、くそっ
⑧ think of A　Ａのことを考える

37

出勤③

あっ、部長、おはようございます

何がおはようですか

あなた、また遅刻ですよ

時間厳守だとあれほど言ったじゃないですか

いったい何度言ったらわかるんですか？

遅れてすみません

でもたった5分遅れただけです

遅刻は遅刻です

言い訳はよしなさい

英語表現

① Look at you! なんだ君、これは（ひどいじゃないか）！
② late 豚 遅刻した
③ punctual 豚 時間を厳守する
④ excuse 言い訳

Going to Work 3

Oh, good morning, boss.

Look at you, saying good morning to me.
①

You're late again.
②

I told you so many times to be **punctual**.
バン(ク)チュアル
③

How many times do I have to tell you that?

I'm sorry that I'm late.

But I was only five minutes late.

Late is late.

Don't give me any excuses.
④

洗濯・掃除

夫はもう会社に着いたころかな…

そろそろ掃除を始めるとするか

そうそう、今日はゴミの日だったわね

急いでゴミを出さなくっちゃ

洗濯物を洗濯機に入れて…

お風呂を掃除して…

掃除機をかけてと…

ああ、疲れた！

主婦の仕事も楽じゃないわね

英語表現

① wonder if …かしらと思う
② get to A A に到着する
③ well さて
④ yeah yes の口語的表現

Doing Laundry and Cleaning

I wonder if my husband got to the office yet.
①　　　　　　　　　　　　②

Well, it's about time for me to start cleaning the house.
③

Yeah, that's right. It's garbage day, today.
④　　　　　　　　　　　　ガーベチ
　　　　　　　　　　　　　⑤

I'd better hurry and take out the garbage.

Put the laundry in the washing machine...

Clean the bathtub...

Vacuum the room...

Gee, I'm exhausted!
イグゾースティド
　　　⑥

Being a housewife is not an easy job.

⑤ garbage 　（台所の）生ごみ
⑥ exhausted 　形 疲れきった、へとへとの

41

赤ちゃんの世話

あれ、赤ちゃんが泣いている

起きちゃったのかしら？

ひかりちゃん、そんなに泣いてどうしたの？

オシッコしたの？

ウンチしたの？

すぐオムツ替えてあげますからね

何、お腹空いたのね

よしよし

おっぱいあげるからね

 英語表現

① pee　オシッコ
② poopy　ウンチ
③ diaper　オムツ
④ I see.　わかった

Taking Care of a Baby

Oh, my baby's crying.

Is she up now?

Hikari, why are you crying?

Did you go pee pee?
①

Did you go poopy?
②

I'll change your diaper ダイ(ア)バァ for you now.
③

Oh, I see. You're hungry.
④

There, there.

Have some milk.

43

ペットの世話

こら、ポチそんなに吠えないで！

お座り！

お手！

よしよし

さあ、エサをあげるからね

モモ、どうしてそんなに暴れてるの？

よしよし

これっ、引っかかないで！

ちょっとおとなしくしなさい！

英語表現
① bark　ほえる
② shake　握手、お手
③ how come（=why）　どうして
④ Knock it off！（不快なことに対して）やめろ！

Taking Care of a Pet

No, Pochi. No barking!
①

Sit!

Shake!
②

Good boy.

Here's your dinner.

Momo, how come you're acting like a maniac?
③

There, there.

Knock it off! Don't scratch!
④

Calm down a little!
⑤

⑤ calm down 落ち着く

会社①

さあ、みんな、仕事を始めよう

仕事をさぼるんじゃないよ

手を抜くなよ

君、書類を提出してくれ

君、この書類に目を通しておいてくれ

君、見積もりを出してくれ

君、このレポートを仕上げてくれ

君、もう1度これをやり直してくれ

君、私にお茶を入れてくれ

英語表現
① get started（＝start）（仕事・活動）を始める
② taking it easy （米俗）一服すること
③ cutting corners　手を抜くこと
④ submit （書類など）を提出する

46

At Work 1

Let's get <u>started</u> working, everyone.
①

No <u>taking it easy</u> on the job.
②

No <u>cutting corners</u>.
③

<u>Submit</u> documents to me, please.
④

Look through these papers for me, please.

クウォウテイション
Give me a <u>quotation</u> on this, please.
⑤

Finish this report, please.

Do this <u>over again</u>, please.
⑥

Bring me some tea, please.

⑤ quotation　見積もり額
⑥ over again　もう1度

会社②

さあ、今日も1日頑張るぞ

とりあえずスケジュールを確認しておこう

なんだかやることがいっぱいあるな…

雑務はさっさと片付けてしまおう

この書類を本社にファックスして…

この書類をホッチキスでとじる…

この書類をコピーして…

あれ、コピー機が動かないぞ

また故障しているよ

英語表現

① All right!　ようし！
② first　副 最初に
③ look like...　…のように見える
④ had better do　…したほうがよい

At Work 2

All right! Let's work hard again today.
①

First I should check my schedule.
②

Looks like I have many things to do...
③

I'd better **polish off** the <ruby>miscellaneous<rt>ミセレイニアス</rt></ruby> things first.
④ ⑤

Fax these documents to the head office...

<ruby>**Staple**<rt>ステイプル</rt></ruby> these papers together...
⑥

Make some copies of these...
⑦

Look at that. Copy machine is not working.

It's **broken** again.
⑧

---

⑤ miscellaneous 形 種々雑多な
⑥ staple をホッチキスでとじる
⑦ make a copy コピーする
⑧ It's broken. (=It has broken.) それは故障してしまった

49

会社③

ねえ、お願いがあるんだけれど？

何？

ちょっと手伝ってくれる？

いますごく忙しいの

やることがたくさんあるのよ

悪いけど他の人に頼んでくれない？

ランチおごるからさ

エッ、それなら話は別よ

何したらいい…？

英語表現

① favor　親切な行い
② give A a hand　A に手を貸す、A を手伝う
③ else　副 その他に
④ now（＝then）副 それなら

At Work 3

Can I ask you a favor?
①

What is it?

Can you give me a hand?
②

I'm very busy now.

I've got so much to do.

I'm sorry but can you ask somebody else?
③

I'll buy you lunch.

Really? Now that's a different story.
④

What do you want me to do for you?

会社④

君、例の契約の件どうなったかね？

それが、キャンセルされてしまいました

いったい君は何をやっているんだ？

あれは大口だったんだよ

できる限りのことはしました

やればいいという問題でもない

君はやる気があるのかね？

いつまでも契約が取れないようなら

君を首にするよ

英語表現

① situation　状況
② in the world　一体全体
③ keep doing　…し続ける
④ fail　失敗する

At Work 4

What is the <u>situation</u> with that contract?
①

Oh, that.　It's been cancelled.

What <u>in the world</u> have you done?
②

That was a big contract.

I tried everything I could.

Trying's not good enough.

Do you have the mind to do your job?

If you <u>keep</u> <u>failing</u> to make contracts,
③　　④

I'll <u>fire</u> you.
⑤

⑤ fire　を解雇する

53

会社⑤

部長、お話し中すみません

ちょっとお邪魔していいですか？

おお、君か

君はいつも頑張ってるね

君のおかげで会社も大儲けだ

残業するのもいいけれど

たまには早く家に帰ってあげなさい

あんまり無理をするなよ

ところで、話とは何だね？

英語表現

① interrupt をじゃまする
② for a little bit 少しの間
③ see を理解する
④ profit 利益

At Work 5

Boss, excuse me for interrupting your
conversation.
①

Can I talk to you for a little bit?
②

Oh, it's you.

I see you always work very hard.
③

The company's making big profits, thanks to
④   ⑤
you.

It's fine to do overtime, but
⑥

why don't you go home early for a change?
⑦

Don't overwork yourself too much.
⑧

Anyway, what was it that you wanted to talk
to me about?

⑤ thanks to A　Ａのおかげで
⑥ overtime　超過勤務
⑦ for a change　気分転換に
⑧ overwork　を働かせすぎる

会社⑥

ああっ、肩がこる

あれ、もうこんな時間？

もうすぐ12時だよ

道理でおなかが空くと思ったよ

おい君、そんなに熱心に仕事するなよ

適当にやりましょうよ

切りをつけてランチに行きましょう

いえ、私はもうちょっと…

君はつきあいが悪いね

英語表現

① stiff 形 こわばった
② Oh boy! おや、まあ！
③ What happened? 何があったのか？
④ take it easy のんびりやる

At Work 6

Gee, my shoulders are stiff.
①

Oh boy, what happened to the time?
②   ③

It's almost noon.

No surprise I'm hungry.

Hey, you.　Don't work so hard.

Let's take it easy.
④

Why don't we take a break and go out for
⑤
lunch?

No, I'll stay here a bit more.

You're not a sociable person, are you?
⑥

⑤ take a break　休憩する
⑥ sociable　形 社交的な

会社⑦

今日は会議があるかしら？

あるって聞いていたけど…

何時からあるのかしら？

たぶん4時からだと思うけど…

皆さん、これから会議です

えっ、まだ2時ですけど…

4時からじゃなかったんですか

時間が変更になりました

皆さん、至急会議室に集まってください

英語表現

① have　を催す、開く、持つ
② meeting　会議
③ Excuse me ?　（語尾を上げ調子で）すみませんがもう1度
　　　　　　　　言ってください

At Work 7

Do we <u>have</u> a <u>meeting</u> today?
　　　　①　　　　②

I heard that we do...

Do you know what time?

I think maybe at 4...

The meeting's starting now, everyone.

<u>Excuse me?</u> But it's still 2 o'clock...
③

We thought the meeting was at 4.

The schedule's been changed.

　　　　　　　　　　　　　　　　カンフ(ェ)レンス
Everyone, come to the <u>conference</u> room, please.
④　　　　　　　　　　　　　　　⑤

④ everyone　みんな
⑤ conference　会議

59

第2章

お昼過ぎ、電話も
あいさつも英語で

電話①

もしもし、太郎？

どちらさんですか？

吉田です

あの〜、電話が遠くて

聞き取りにくいんです

もう少し大きい声で話していただけますか？

吉田というものですが、

鈴木太郎さんをお願いしたいのですが…

間違い電話です

英語表現

① um　うむ、えーっと（ためらいの声）
② connection　（電話の）接続
③ so　だから
④ louder　（loud の比較級）副 より大声で（more loudly より口

Telephone 1

Hello, is this Taro?

Who's this, please?

It's Yoshida calling.

<u>Um</u>, we have a bad <u>connection</u>,
①   ②

<u>so</u> I can't hear you very well.
③

Would you speak a little <u>louder</u>?
④

This is Yoshida calling.

<u>I'd like to speak</u> to Mr. Taro Suzuki, please...
⑤

You have the wrong number.

語的)
⑤ would like to do　…したいのですが

63

電話②

もしもし、Ｚオフィスですか？

はい、そうですが…

社長の本田さんをお願いします

はい、私です

どちらさまですか？

Ａ証券会社の豊田と申します

こ用件は何でしょうか？

はい、株式投資の件で電話しました

まったく興味がありません

英語表現
① May I...? 私は…してもよろしいですか？
② securities （ふつう複数形で）有価証券
③ stock 株式
④ investment 投資

Telephone 2

Hello, is this Z Office?

Yes. May I help you?

May I speak to President Honda, please?
①

This is Honda speaking.

May I ask who's calling, please?

This is Toyota from A Securities Corporation.
セキュ(ア)リティズ
②

How may I help you?

I'm calling about stock investments.
インヴェストゥメンツ
③ ④

I have no interest in it at all.
⑤ ⑥

⑤interest　興味
⑥at all　（否定文で）少しも…（ない）

65

電話③

もしもしR会社です

加藤さんをお願いしたいのですが…

どちらの加藤におかけですか？

たぶん営業部だったと思います

少々お待ちください

営業部には加藤という

名のものはおりません

何かのお間違えではありませんか？

そんなはずないと思うんだけれど…

英語表現

① department 部署
② believe （きっと…だと）思う
③ One moment. （＝Wait a moment.） 少々お待ちください
④ be sure (that)... きっと…だと思う

Telephone 3

Hello, R Corporation.

May I speak to Mr. Kato, please?

Kato from which department?
①

I believe he's in the sales department.
②

One moment, please.
③

We don't have anybody

whose name is Kato in the sales department.

I'm sorry, but are you sure you're not mistaken?
④   ⑤   ⑥

I don't think I'm mistaken...

⑤ be mistaken　間違っている
⑥ mistaken　形 間違った

電話④

もしもし、ご用件は何でしょうか？

Ｗ会社の田中と申します

経理課の佐藤さんをお願いします

ちょっとお待ちください

電話を経理課に回します

佐藤さん、田中さんという方から電話です

「いない」と言っておいてくれ…

すみません、いま、席を外しているみたいです

たぶん社内にはいると思うのですが…

英語表現

① accounting　会計
② hold　（状態などを）保つ
③ transfer　を移す
④ be on the phone　電話に出ている

Telephone 4

Hello, how may I help you?

This is Tanaka from W Corporation speaking.

May I speak to Mr. Sato in the accounting
①
section, please?

Please hold.
②

I'll transfer your call to the accounting
③
section.

Mr. Sato, Mr. Tanaka's on the phone for you.
④

Tell him I'm NOT at my desk...

I'm sorry, but he's away from his desk right
⑤
now.

オール ゾゥ
Although I think he's in the office...
⑥

⑤ away from A　A から離れて
⑥ although　…だけれども

69

電話⑤

もしもし、先ほど電話した田中ですが…

すみません、いま、佐藤は電話中です

このままお待ちになりますか？

じゃ、待ってます

すみません、まだ終わらないみたいです

そうですか

どうしようかな…

それでは後でかけ直します

何度も何度もすみません

英語表現

① a while　少しの時間
② be afraid (that)...　残念ですが…
③ on the line　電話に出て
④ I see.　なるほど

Telephone 5

Hello, this is Tanaka again. I called just a
while ago...
①

I'm afraid that Sato's on the phone right now.
②

Would you like to hold?

Yes, I'll hold.

I'm sorry, but he's still on the line.
③

I see.
④

Let me think...

I'll call him back later, then.

I'm sorry for your trouble.
⑤

⑤ trouble　迷惑

電話⑥

もしもし、佐藤さん電話終わりましたか？

申し訳ありません

電話が終ってすぐ出かけたみたいです

どちらに出かけられたのでしょうか？

さあ、それがよくわからないのですが…

こちらから電話するように伝えましょうか？

ええ、お願いします

電話番号をお願いします

私の番号は090-1234-5678です

英語表現

① done 形 済んだ
② It seems (that) A does　A は…するように思われる
③ as soon as...　…するとすぐに
④ hang up　（電話）を切る

Telephone 6

Hello, is Mr. Sato done speaking on the
① phone?

I'm very sorry.

It seems he left the office as soon as he
② ③
hung up the phone.
④

Do you know where he went?

Well. No, I don't...

Would you like me to tell him to call you
⑤
back?

Yes, please.

May I have your number, please?

My number is 090-1234-5678.

⑤ call back A　A に電話をかけ返す

電話⑦

あのう、佐藤さん戻られましたか？

彼はまだ外出中です

まだですか…

彼は何時ごろ戻ってこられますか？

すぐ戻ってくると思うのですが…

さっきから何度も電話してるんです

伝言を伝えておいてください

今回の契約はなかったことにしてくれと

はあ、わかりました

英語表現

① out 副 外出して
② about 副 およそ
③ several times 何回か
④ at this time 今度の

74

Telephone 7

Is Mr. Sato back in the office?

He's still out.
①

Still out...

About what time will he be coming back?
②

I believe he'll be back soon...

I've called him several times, now.
③

Would you give him a message for me?

I'd like to cancel our contract at this time.
④

Oh, I see.
⑤

⑤ I see.　わかった

75

電話⑧

あら、話に夢中になっていたら

もうこんな時間だわ

随分長電話したわね

そろそろ電話切らないと…

久しぶりに電話できて楽しかったわ

私もよ

それじゃ、またね

電話ありがとう

また電話するわ

英語表現

① (Oh,) my goodness!　なんということだ！
② be engrossed in A　A に夢中になっている
③ quite　副 かなり
④ had better do...　…したほうがいい

Telephone 8

①My goodness, we were so engrossed in the
conversation. ②

Look at the time.

We talked for ③quite a long time on the
phone, didn't we?

I'd better hang up the phone now...
④

Nice talking to you after such a long time.
⑤

Me, too.

Talk to you later.
⑥

Thanks for calling.

I'll call you again.

⑤ Nice talking (=It is nice talking)　話しできてよかった
⑥ Talk to you later.　それじゃ、また（決まり文句）

あいさつ①

やあ、山田君、こんにちは

お久しぶり

本当に久しぶりだね

元気してましたか？

ああ、そちらこそどう？

まあまあってところかな

でもこんなところで会うなんて奇遇だね

本当に

どう、ちょっとお茶でもしない？

英語表現

① Long time no see.／I haven't seen you for a long time.
　久しぶり（カジュアルな表現）
② It's been a while.（＝It's been a long time.）久しぶりですね
③ Fancy doing …するなんて（驚きだ）

Saying Hello 1

Hey, Mr. Yamada. Hello.

Long time no see.
①

Really. It's been a while.
②

How have you been?

Fine. How about you?

I'm OK.

Fancy meeting you here.
③

<ruby>アブソルートゥリィ</ruby>
Absolutely.
④

How about joining me for a cup of tea?

④ absolutely 　副 まったくそのとおり

あいさつ②

まあ、中村さん、こんにちは

調子のほうはいかがですか？

とてもいいですよ

見るからにお元気そうですものね

小林さんはいかがですか？

それがあまり良くありませんの

どうかなさいましたの？

ええ、ちょっと体の調子が良くなくてね

これから医者に診てもらいに行くところなんです

英語表現

① look A （外観が）A に見える
② What about...? …はいかがですか？
③ actually 圖 実際には
④ feel A A の感じがする

Saying Hello 2

Oh, hi, Mrs. Nakamura.

How are you feeling?

I'm feeling fine.

You look good.
①

What about you, Mrs. Kobayashi?
②

Actually, not too good.
③

Something wrong?

Yes, I'm not feeling too good, actually.
④

I'm on the way to see a doctor.
⑤   ⑥

⑤ on the way (to A)　（Aへ行く）途中で
⑥ see a doctor　医者に診てもらう

81

久しぶりの再会①

おい、水野、おれだよ！

えっ、誰？

おれだよ、忘れたのか？

高校の同級生の水谷だよ

水谷か!?

いや～っ、懐かしいね

お前随分変わったな

ぜんぜんわからなかったよ

しかし相変わらず元気そうじゃないか

英語表現
① quite a bit　かなり多く
② I have no idea.　私にはわからない
③ as good as A　A も同然で

Reunion 1

Hey, Mizuno! It's me!

Excuse me? Who are you?

It's me. Don't you remember me?

Mizutani, your high school classmate.

Mizutani!?

Wow, it's been a long time.

You've changed quite a bit.
　　　　　　　　①

I had no idea it was you.
②

Anyway, you're looking as good as before.
　　　　　　　　　　　③

久しぶりの再会②

お前のほうは元気かい？

悪くもなく良くもないってところかな

何か変わったことあった？

とくにないよ

ところでお前いま何やってるんだ？

おれか？

弁護士をやってる

うそ、本当かよ！

劣等生だったお前が…？

英語表現

① I'd (＝I would)
② since 副 それ以来、その後
③ particularly 副 とくに
④ No kidding!（＝You're kidding!） うそー、ご冗談でしょ！

Reunion 2

How have you been?

I'd say not too bad and not too good.
①

Has anything changed since school?
②

Not particularly.
③
パティキュラリィ

By the way, what do you do, now?

Me?

I'm a lawyer.

No kidding!
④

You with such a poor performance at
school...?
⑤

⑤ performance 成績

85

久しぶりの再会③

まあ、直美、お久しぶり

ご無沙汰してます

まあ、智子じゃない

こんなところで会えるなんて驚き！

でも相変わらずあなたはキレイね

あらそう？

そうでもないけど…

でもお世辞でもうれしいわ

ところで最近どうしてた？

英語表現

① What a surprise!　ああ驚いた！
② as...as ever　相変わらず…
③ flatter　のお世辞を言う
④ these days　このごろ

Reunion 3

Wow, Naomi, it's been a while.

Good to see you again.

My god, it's you, Tomoko.

<u>What a surprise</u> seeing you here!
①

You look <u>as beautiful as ever.</u>
②

You think so?

Not that beautiful...

I know you're only <u>flattering</u> me, but I'm
③ フラタリング
glad.

By the way, how're things going <u>these days</u>
④
for you?

87

別れのあいさつ①

いま時間ある？

それが私いま急いでいるの

これから行かなくてはいけないところがあるのよ

せっかく再会したんだもの

また近いうちに会わない？

ええ、ぜひ会いましょう

これが私の連絡先

あとで電話してくれない

8時以降ならいつでもいるから

英語表現

① have got　を持っている
② in a hurry　急いで
③ since　（理由を表して）…ので
④ get together　集まる

Saying Goodbye 1

Have you got time?
①

Actually, I'm in a hurry.
②

I have to go some place now.

Since we met here again,
③

shall we get together again sometime soon?
④　　　　　　　　⑤

Sure, why not?
⑥

This is my contact number.

Will you call me later?

I'm usually available anytime after 8 o'clock.
⑦

⑤ sometime 副 いつか
⑥ Why not? いいですよ
⑦ available 形 手があいている

89

別れのあいさつ②

せっかく会えて残念だけど

いま時間がないんだ

もう行かなくっちゃ

これで失敬するよ

中村、無茶をするなよ

お前こそ

気をつけてね

元気でね

君の奥さんによろしく言っておいてくれ

英語表現

① although　…だけれども
② get doing　…し始める
③ take it easy　「気楽に」というニュアンス
④ Good luck!　幸運を祈ります、ごきげんよう!

Saying Goodbye 2

Although we just met again,
オールゾウ
①

I don't have time now.

I have to go now.

I must get going.
②

Nakamura, take it easy.
③

Same to you.

Take care.

Good luck to you.
④

Tell your wife I said hello.

第3章

午後のひととき、まだ英語でいける！

天気のあいさつ①

鈴木さん、今日はいい天気ですね

ええ、本当にいい天気です

空は快晴ですし

気持ちがいいですね

天気予報は雨だと

言ってたんですけどね

天気予報も当たらないものですね

でもこの様子だと、

今日は暑くなりそうですよ

英語表現

① lovely 形 快い
② make A do A に…させる
③ great 形 すばらしい
④ be supposed to do …するものと考えられている

Talking about the Weather 1

Mr. Suzuki, what a nice day, today, don't you think?

Yes. Really a <u>lovely</u> day.
①

The sky's clear,

and <u>makes</u> me <u>feel</u> <u>great</u>.
② ③

It <u>was supposed to rain</u> today
④

アコーディング
and <u>according to the weather forecast</u>, but
⑤

I guess the <u>forecast</u>'s not always right, <u>eh</u>?
⑥ エイ ⑦

But from the <u>look</u> of the sky,
⑧

<u>it seems like</u> it will be a hot day, today.
⑨

⑤ according to A　A によれば
⑥ forecast　（天気の）予報
⑦ Eh?　ねっ？
⑧ look　様子
⑨ it seems like...　…のようだ

95

天気のあいさつ②

今日も空がどんよりしていますね

この様子だとまた雨が降りそうですよ

そんな感じですね

いつまで雨の日が続くのでしょうね

もうかれこれ2週間続いていますよ

早く晴れてほしいものです

しかも今日はいつになく風も強いし

とても寒いです

お体にお気をつけください

英語表現

① looks like A　Aになりそうだ
② sure　劚 きっと
③ wonder　…かしらと思う
④ nearly　劚 ほとんど

Talking about the Weather 2

The sky's cloudy again today.

It looks like rain.
①

It sure does.
②

I wonder how long we'll have rainy days like
③
this.

It's been nearly two weeks now.
④

I wish it would be sunny soon.
⑤

What's more, it's unusually windy today, and
⑥   ⑦

very chilly.

Take care of yourself.

⑤ I wish A would be... A が…であってほしい
⑥ what's more　そのうえ、おまけに
⑦ unusually　副 異常に

天気のあいさつ③

昨日までは過ごしやすい天気だったけど

今日はやけに暑いね

そりゃそうですよ

気温は30度を超えているんですからね

何、30度超えているんですか?

道理で暑いと思った

しかも湿気が多いから

ムシムシするよ

しかたありませんよ

英語表現

① comfortable 形 快適な
② awfully 副 ひどく
③ quite 副 まったく
④ temperature 温度

Talking about the Weather 3

We had such comfortable weather until
yesterday, but
① カンファタブル

it's awfully hot today.
② オーフリィ

Quite so.
③

The temperature's over 30 degrees.
④ テンペラチ(ュ)ア ⑤

What, over 30?

Now I know why it's so hot.

And, because the humidity's so high,
⑥ ヒュ(ー)ミディティ

the air feels so sticky to me.
⑦

Nothing you can do about it.

⑤ degree　度
⑥ humidity　湿度
⑦ sticky　形 蒸し暑い

天気のあいさつ④

わあ、すごい雪だ

一晩でこんなに雪が積もってる

いつまで雪が降るのかな

この調子だとまだまだ降りそうね

都会でこれほどの雪はめずらしいね

20年ぶりの大雪みたいよ

ねえ、あなた大変申し訳ないけど…

これから雪かきしてくださらない？

このままじゃ外にも出られないわ

英語表現

① pile up　たまる
② keep doing　…し続ける
③ a while　しばらくの間
④ uncommon　形 めずらしい

Talking about the Weather 4

Wow, look at that heavy snow.

It <u>piled up</u> so high overnight.
①

I wonder how long it'll <u>keep snowing</u>.
②

It may be <u>a while</u> from the look of it.
③

It's <u>uncommon</u> to see this much snow in the
④　アンカモン
city, isn't it?

It's the heaviest snow we've had in twenty
years.

Hey, honey, <u>I'm sorry to bother you, but</u>
⑤

can you <u>shovel</u> the snow for me now?
⑥　シャヴ(ェ)ル

I can't <u>get out of</u> the house like this.
⑦

⑤ I'm sorry to bother you, but...　お手数だけど…
⑥ shovel　をシャベルですくう
⑦ get out of A　A から出る

101

日時をたずねる①

つかぬことを聞きますが…

はい、何でしょう？

今日は何日でしたか？

5月5日です

今日はこどもの日なんだ

それから今日は何曜日でしたっけ？

月曜日です

ああ、そうでしたよね

年を取ると物忘れが激しくて…

英語表現

① sure　副 もちろん、いいとも
② What's the date today?　今日は何月何日？
③ What day is it today?　今日は何曜日？
④ forgetful　形 忘れっぽい

Asking the Time and Date 1

Can I ask you a question?

Sure, what is it?
①

What's the date today?
②

It's May 5.

It's Children's Day today.

And, what day is it today?
③

It's Monday.

Ah, that's right.

I've become forgetful because of my age, you
know...
④   ⑤

⑤ you know …でね

日時をたずねる②

すみません、時間をお伺いしていいですか？

いま何時ですか？

いまですか…？

えっと、もうすぐ正午です

正確には何時ですか？

正確にですか…？

11時45分です

12時15分前ですね

あと15分で12時ですか…

英語表現

① the time　時刻（time の前に the をつける）
② exactly　副 正確に
③ I see.　なるほど
④ quarter　15分

104

Asking the Time and Date 2

Excuse me. May I ask the time?
①

What time is it now?

Now...?

Well, it's almost noon.

What time is it, exactly?
②

Exactly...?

It's 11:45.

I see. It's quarter to 12.
③   ④   ⑤

15 more minutes to 12, eh...?

⑤ to　（時刻の）…前

駅で①

自由ヶ丘に行きたいのですが…

どの電車に乗ればいいのですか？

まずJR線に乗ってくだい

そして渋谷で降りてください

駅を出て

それから東急東横線に乗りかえてください

東横線の駅は地下にあります

いくらかかりますか？

いや、そこまではわかりません

英語表現
① take 　に乗る
② get off 　降りる
③ get out of A 　Aから出る
④ transfer 　乗りかえる

At the Station 1

I'd like to go to Jiyugaoka.

Which train should I take?
①

First, take the JR Line.

And get off at Shibuya Station.
②

You need to get out of the station
③

to transfer to the Tokyu Toyoko Line.
④

Toyoko Line is underground.
⑤

How much is the ticket?

Well, I don't know.

⑤ underground 地下

駅で②

渋谷はこの電車で行けますか？

いいえ、行けませんよ

反対側のプラットホームから乗ってください

渋谷はこの電車でいいですよね？

ええ、この電車でいいですよ

渋谷まであと何駅ありますか？

次の次です

私も降りますので

いっしょに降りましょう

英語表現

① take　を連れて行く
② won't（＝will not）
③ opposite　形 向こう側の
④ get off　降りる

At the Station 2

Will this train take me to Shibuya?
①

No, it won't.
②

You need to take a train from the opposite
platform.
③

Is this the train to Shibuya?

Yes, it is.

How many stations are there before Shibuya?

One after the next.

I'm getting off there, so
④   ⑤

let's get off together.
⑥

⑤ so それで
⑥ let's (=let us) …しよう

バス停で

市民病院に行きたいのですが…

バスは何番線から乗ればいいのですか？

5番線から乗ってください

市民病院までいくらかかりますか？

250円です

それでは切符を1枚ください

次のバスは何時に来ますか？

いま11時25分ですから…

あと5分くらいしたら来ます

英語表現
① I'd like to do　…したいのですが（柔らかい言い方）
② How much...?　いくら？
③ have　を受け取る
④ so　だから

At the Bus Stop

I'd like to go to the city hospital...
① ‾‾‾‾‾‾‾‾‾

From which platform should I take a bus?

Please take a bus from Platform 5.

How much is it to the city hospital?
② ‾‾‾‾‾‾

It's 250 yen.

Can I have one ticket, please?
③ ‾‾‾‾

When is the next bus coming?

It's 11:25 now..., so
④ ‾‾

in about 5 minutes.
⑤ ‾‾

⑤ in　…の後に

タクシー①

タクシー乗り場はどこですか？

タクシー乗り場ですか？

ほら、あそこです

あっ、あそこですね

わかりました

荷物をトランクに入れていただけますか？

これは私が持っています

お客さん、どちらまで？

この住所までお願いします

英語表現

① over there　向こうに
② luggage　手荷物
③ hold on to A　A をしっかり持つ
④ sir は男性に対して、女性には ma'am を用いる

Taxi 1

Where's the taxi stand?

Taxi stand?

It's over there.
①

Oh, over there.

I see.

Could you put my luggage in the trunk?
②

I'll hold on to this.
③

Where to, sir?
④

To this address, please.

タクシー②

C町までいくらかかりますか？

そうですね、3000円はかかりますよ

案外かかるんですね

とにかく急いでいるんです

できるだけ早く行ってください

お客さん、そろそろC町です

そこで止めてください

おいくらですか？

お釣りは取っておいてください

英語表現

① Let me see.（＝Let's see.）　ええと
② cost　（金額・費用）がかかる
③ that　副 そんなに
④ in a hurry　急いで

Taxi 2

How much is it to C Town?

Let me see, it's about 3,000 yen.
①

It costs that much, eh.
②   ③

Anyway, I'm in a hurry.
④

Take me there as fast as possible, please.
⑤

We're almost there, C Town, sir.

Stop the car there, please.

How much?

Please keep the change.
⑥

⑤ as...as possible　できるだけ…に
⑥ change　釣り銭

道をたずねる①

あれ、道に迷ってしまったな…

すみません、ちょっと道をお尋ねしたいのですが

私はこの地図のどこにいますか？

どちらに行きたいんですか？

K会館に行きたいのですが…

それならここのすぐ近くです

この道をずっとまっすぐに行ってください

2つ目の角に薬局があります

その角を左に曲がったら、すぐです

英語表現

① lost 形 迷った
② directions 道順
③ be headed for A A に向かう
④ go on （先へ）進む

Asking Directions 1

Oh no, I'm lost...
①

Excuse me. Can I ask you for directions?
②

Where are we on this map?

Where are you headed?
③

I'd like to go to K Hall...

It's very close to here.

Go straight on this road.
④

There'll be a drugstore at the second corner.
⑤

You'll find K Hall right after you make a left
⑥
turn at that corner.

⑤ There'll be (＝There will be)
⑥ right 圓 すぐに

道をたずねる②

すみません、ちょっとお伺いします

Hホテルはどこにありますか？

さっきから探し回っているのですが…

Hホテルですか？

ええっと、どこだったかな…？

そうそう、あそこだ

ほら、向こうに高いビルが見えるでしょ

たぶんあそこですよ

間違ってたらゴメンね

英語表現

① look for A　Aを探す
② quite　副 実際
③ umm　ええっと（ためらいの声）
④ That's right.　そのとおりだ

Asking Directions 2

Excuse me. Could you help me with directions?

Where can I find H Hotel?

I've been looking for it for quite some time...
①   ②

H Hotel?

Umm, where was it...?
③

Yeah, that's right. It's over there.
④

Can you see the tall building in that direction?

I think that's it.

I'm sorry if I am wrong.

道をたずねる③

Ｒ公園へ行く道を教えていただけませんか？

私に聞かれてもわかりません

私ここに来たの初めてなんです

お役に立てずすみません

私、知ってます

Ｒ公園に行かれるんですよね

３本目の道を右に曲がって

ずっと真っ直ぐ行ってください

300ｍくらい先にＲ公園があります

英語表現

① the way to A　Ａへ行く道
② be of help　役に立つ
③ (Is that) right?　そうなの？
④ away　副 離れて

Asking Directions 3

Can you tell me the way to R Park?
①

I'm sorry but I don't know.

This is my first time to come to this place.

I'm sorry I can't be of any help.
②

I know the way.

You're going to R Park, right?
③

Make a right turn at the third street,

and go straight on that street.

R Park is about 300 m away.
④

第4章

外出中も
英語ですごそう

訪問①

ごめんください

まあ、山口さん、いらっしゃい

よく来てくださいました

お招きくださってありがとう

いえ、こちらこそ来てくれてありがとう

さあ、どうぞ中に入ってください

いいお住まいですね

そんなこともないです

足元に気をつけてくださいね

英語表現

① come on in　さあさあ、お入り
② invite　を招待する
③ Not at all.　どういたしまして
④ Go ahead.　さあ、どうぞ

Visiting 1

Hello.

Hi, Ms. Yamaguchi, come on in.
①

Thank you for coming.

Thank you for inviting me.
②

Not at all. I'm glad that you came.
③

Go ahead and come inside.
④

Nice house.

Not at all, thank you.
⑤

Watch your step.
⑥

⑤at all （否定文で）少しも…（ない）
⑥watch に注意する

訪問②

遠慮せずに気楽にしてください

ところで何か飲み物はいかがですか？

おかまいなく

でもやはり何か飲み物をいただこうかな…

のどが渇いてしまっていて…

何がいいですか？

オレンジジュースはありますか？

すみません、オレンジジュースはないんです

じゃ、何でもいいです

英語表現

① trouble　に手数をかける
② on second thought　（すぐに考えを変えて）やはり
③ thirsty　圏 のどが渇いた
④ then　圏 それでは

Visiting 2

Make yourself at home.

So, what would you like to drink?

Don't trouble yourself.
①

On second thought, maybe I'll have something...
②

I'm thirsty...
③

What would you like?

Do you have orange juice?

I'm sorry I don't have orange juice.

Then, anything's fine.
④

紹介

杉山さん、私の上司を紹介します

こちら私の上司の松本さんです

こちらは私の友人の杉山さんです

はじめまして

こちらこそはじめまして

お会いできてうれしいです

ところで以前どこかでお会いしたことありませんか？

いえ、私たちは初対面だと思います

どこかでお会いしたような気がするんですが…

英語表現

① let me do　私に…させてください
② Nice to meet you.（＝It is nice to meet you.）　はじめまして
③ You know what?　あのう
④ feel like...　…のような気がする

Introductions

Mr. Sugiyama, let me introduce my boss to you.
①

This is my boss, Mr. Matsumoto.

This is my friend, Mr. Sugiyama.

Nice to meet you.
②

Nice to meet you, too.

I'm glad to see you.

③You know what? Have we met somewhere before?

No, I think this is the first time.

I feel like I've met you somewhere before...
④

写真

ねえ、写真撮らない？

ああ、ぜひ写真を撮ろう

じゃ、私が写真を撮ってあげる

もうちょっと下がって

ちょっと下がりすぎ

もう少し近寄って

はい笑って…

撮るわよ

カシャ！

英語表現

① hey　ねえ（親しい間柄での呼びかけ）
② take a picture　写真を撮る
③ Why not?　うん、そうしよう
④ closer　（close の比較級）圖 より近くに

Taking Pictures

Hey, do you want to take some pictures?
① ②

Why not? Let's take some pictures.
③

Well, I'll take pictures of you.

Step back a little.

That's too much.

Come in closer.
④

OK, smile...

Are you ready?

Click!

おいとま

あれ、もう7時

そろそろ帰らないと…

もう帰っちゃうんですか？

他に色々と用事があるものですから…

そうですか

それは残念です

これで失礼します

ぜひまた来てくださいね

ええ、また遊びに来ます

英語表現

① My goodness.　おやおや、あらまあ（軽い驚き）
② had better do　…したほうがよい
③ get doing　…し始める
④ already　副　もう

Heading Home

My goodness, it's almost 7.
①

I'd better get going...
②   ③

You're leaving **already**?
④

I have other **stuff** to do...
⑤

I see.

That's too bad.
⑥

I'll be going now.

Do come and see me again.

デフィニトゥリィ
Definitely. I will come again.
⑦

⑤ stuff   物事
⑥ That's too bad.   それは残念です
⑦ definitely   副 確かに

ファーストフード

いらっしゃいませ！

チーズバーガー１つとコーラ２つください

それからホットドッグを１つ

その他に何か？

それだけです

こちらでお召し上がりですか

それともお持ち帰りですか？

こちらです

８ドル50セントです

英語表現
① Can I...?　…しましょうか？
② anything　（疑問文で）何か
③ (Do you want)anything else?　何か他のものが欲しいですか？
④ That's it.　そうだ、それでおしまいだ

Fast Food

Can I help you?
①

Can I get a cheeseburger and two cokes?

And one hotdog.

Anything else?
②③

That's it.
④

Are these for here,
⑤

or to go?

For here.

That'll be 8 dollars and 50 cents, please.

⑤ For here, or to go?　ここで召し上がりますか、お持ち帰り
ですか？

ショッピング①

あなたショッピングに付き合ってくださらない？

たまには2人で銀座をブラブラしましょうよ

わあ～、すごい人ごみだ！

さすがに銀座ね

ねえ、このお店素敵ね

入りましょうよ

いらっしゃいませ

何かお探しですか？

いえ、ただ見て回っているだけですから…

英語表現

① Will you...?　…してくれませんか？
② hang out　うろつく
③ for a change　気分転換に
④ in particular（＝particularly）　とくに

136

Shopping 1

Will you go shopping with me?
①

Let's **hang out** in Ginza, the two of us, **for a**
②
change.
③

Wow, look at the crowd!

イクスペクティド
It's Ginza, as was **expected.**

Hey, this looks like a nice boutique.

Let's go inside.

Can I help you?

パティキュラァ
Looking for something **in particular?**
④

ブラウズィング
No, we're just **browsing...**
⑤

⑤ browse （商店で）品物をのぞく

137

ショッピング②

何かご用がありましたらお申し付けください

わかりました

ねえ、あなた、これ見て

素敵なパンツね

私に似合うかしら

ちょっと試着していい？

もちろん、結構です

どうぞ試着してください

試着室はどこですか？

英語表現

① look at A　Aを見る
② pants　ズボン（trousers のくだけた言い方）
③ look A　（外観が）Aに見える
④ try on A　Aを試しに身につけてみる

Shopping 2

Let me know if you need any help.

We will.

Hey, honey, look at this.
①

Nice pants.
②

I wonder if they look nice on me.
③

Can I try these on?
④

Certainly, you can.
⑤

Please try them on.

Where is the fitting room?

⑤ certainly 副 いいですとも、もちろん

139

ショッピング③

これちょっと小さくて窮屈だわ

これより大きいサイズない？

サイズはおいくつですか？

ウエストは65センチかしら

ちょっとお待ちください

これはいかがでしょうか？

これならちょうどピッタリ

でも少し派手過ぎない？

そんなことないですよ

英語表現
① tight 厖 きつい
② One moment.（＝Wait a moment.） ちょっと待ってください
③ What about A? Ａはいかがですか？
④ flashy 厖 派手な

Shopping 3

They're a little small and tight on me.
①

Do you have them in a larger size?

May I ask your size?

65 cm in the waist, maybe.

One moment, please.
②

What about these?
③

They're just the right size.

But don't you think they're a little too flashy?
フ ラ シィ
④

Not at all.
⑤

⑤ at all （否定文で）少しも…（ない）

141

ショッピング④

よくお似合いですよ

もう１つのほうはどうかしら？

これはちょっと地味ね

ねえ、あなたどう思う？

どっちがいい？

さっきのほうがいいね

やっぱりそう思う？

じゃあ、これいただこうかしら

かしこまりました

英語表現

① look good on A　A に似合う
② How about A?　A はいかがですか？
③ conservative　形 地味な

Shopping 4

They look good on you.
①

How about the other one?
②

These are a little too conservative, aren't they?
③ コンサ～ヴァティブ

What do you think, honey?

Which one do you like better?

I like the other one.

You think so, too, eh?

Then, I'll take this one.

Thank you very much.

ショッピング⑤

カバン売り場はどこですか？

４階です

ハンドバッグが欲しいのですが…

右から３番目のものを見せていただけますか？

これですか？

いえ、その隣の赤いものです

そうそう、それ

この同じ型で白いのありますか？

ちょっと在庫を見てきます

英語表現

① department （デパートの）売り場
② be looking for A　A を探している
③ one （前に出た名詞の繰り返しをさけて）もの
④ in　…の

Shopping 5

Where can I find the handbag department?
①

It's on the fourth floor.

I'm looking for a handbag...
②

Could you show me the third one from the right?
③

This one?

No, the red one next to that.

Yes, that's it.

Do you have the same design in white?
④

Let me go check in our stock for you.

ショッピング⑥

ありました

どうでしょうか？

気にいったわ

これいただくわ

ところでお値段いくらだったかしら？

2万5000円です

そんなにするの？

ちょっと高いわね

もう少し安くしていただけない？

英語表現

① How is that?　どうですか？
② take（=buy）　を買う
③ That much?　そんなにたくさん？
④ a little　少し

Shopping 6

I found one for you.

How's that?
①

I like it.

I'll take it.
②

By the way, how much is it?

It's 25,000 yen.

That much?
③

A little expensive.
④

Can you make it a little cheaper?
⑤

⑤ make A B　AをBにする

ショッピング⑦

これプレゼント用に包んでいただけますか？

箱に入れてくださいね

手数をかけてすみませんね

お支払いは現金ですか、それともカードですか？

カードでお願いします

このカード使えますか？

当店では扱っておりません

じゃ、このビザカードでお願い

分割払いはできますか？

英語表現

① gift-wrap を贈り物用に包装する
② put...in A …をAに入れる
③ take を受け取る
④ accept を受け取る

Shopping 7

Can you gift-wrap this for me?
①

Put it in a box, please.
②

I'm sorry to trouble you.

Would you like to pay in cash or by credit card?

Credit card, please.

Do you take this card?
③

No, we don't accept that card.
④

Then, the VISA card, please.

インストールメンツ
Can I purchase in installments?
⑤

⑤ in installments　分割払いで

美容室①

お客様、今日はどのようにいたしましょうか？

そうね、どうしたらいいかしら？

髪が傷んでいますので、

今回はカットだけになされてはいかがでしょうか？

あなたの言うとおりにするわ

長さはどのくらいにしますか？

このくらいの長さだけ切ってください

短く切りすぎないでね

あとはあなたにおまかせするわ

英語表現

① be damaged　損害を与えられる
② How about A?　A にしませんか？
③ for　…に関しては
④ as　…のとおりに

Beauty Shop 1

How would like it done today, ma'am?

Let me see, what do you think?

Your hair <u>is damaged</u>, so
　　　　　①

<u>how about</u> just <u>a haircut</u> <u>for</u> today?
②　　　　　　　　　③

I'll do <u>as</u> you have suggested.
　　　　④

What about the <u>length</u>?
　　　　　　　　⑤
（レング(ク)ス）

Cut about this much.

<u>Don't make it</u> too short, <u>though</u>.
　　　⑥　　　　　　　　　⑦
（ゾウ）

<u>I'll leave everything else up to you</u>.
　　⑧

⑤length　長さ
⑥make A B　AをBにする
⑦though　副でも、けれど
⑧leave... (up) to A　…をAにゆだねる

151

美容室②

どのようなヘアースタイルにしましょうか？

写真を持って来たんだけれど…

こんな感じにしてくれない

パーマをかけないといけませんね

それから髪をお染めするんですね？

見本をお持ちします

どの色がいいですか？

この茶色がお似合いだと思いますが…

あなたを信頼してその茶色にするわ

英語表現

① have A done　A を…してもらう、させる
② perm　にパーマをかける
③ would like A done　A を…してもらいたい
④ (Is that) right?　これでいいんですよね？

Beauty Shop 2

What kind of hairstyle would you like?

I brought a picture with me...

Can you make it like this?

I have to <u>have</u> your hair <u>permed</u>.
　　　　　①　　　　　　　②

And <u>you'd</u> like your hair <u>colored</u>, too, <u>right</u>?
　　　③　　　　　　　　　　　④

I'll show you some color samples.

What color would you like?

I think this brown's good for you...

I <u>trust</u> you, so I'll take the brown.
　①

⑤ trust 　を信頼する

153

歯科医院

歯が痛むんです

いつから痛いんですか？

2～3日前からです

ちょっと歯を見せてください

ここですね？

かなり大きな虫歯ですね

他にも何カ所か虫歯がありますよ

また歯ぐきが歯槽膿漏ですね

治療に時間がかかりそうですよ

英語表現

① toothache　歯痛
② take a look at A　A を一目見る
③ cavity　（虫歯でできた）歯の空洞
④ pyorrhea　歯槽膿漏

Dentist

I have a toothache.
①

How long have you had the toothache?

About 2-3 days.

Let me take a look at your teeth.
②

This one, isn't it?

You have quite a big cavity.
③ キャヴィティ

There're a few other cavities, too.

And also pyorrhea.
④ パイオリーア

You might have to spend some time in treatment.
⑤   ⑥   ⑦   ⑧

⑤ might …かも知れない
⑥ spend を使う、費やす
⑦ some time しばらく
⑧ treatment 治療

155

病院①

どうなさいましたか？

ええ、風邪をひいたみたいです

咳が止まりませんし

鼻水も出ます

お腹の調子もよくありません

下痢が続いています

関節も痛みます

最近インフルエンザが流行ってますからね

注射を打っておきましょう

英語表現
① stop doing　…することをやめる
② runny　形 鼻水が出やすい
③ diarrhea　下痢
④ joint　関節

At the Doctor 1

What can I do for you?

Um, I think I have a cold.

I can't stop coughing,
①

and I have a runny nose.
②

My stomach doesn't feel right either.

I've had diarrhea for a while.
③

My joints hurt, too.
④

Influenza's been going around these days, so
⑤

let me give you an injection.
⑥

⑤ go around　（病気が）広がる
⑥ injection　注射

病院②

どんな症状ですか？

夜なかなか寝付けません

食欲もありません

時々めまいがします

動悸もします

またずっと便秘が続いています

そのせいだと思うのですが、

痔なんです

あらあら、それは大変ですね…

英語表現

① symptom　症状
② appetite　食欲
③ dizzy　形 めまいがする
④ palpitation　（しばしば複数形で）動悸

At the Doctor 2

What are your symptoms?
①

I've been having a difficult time sleeping at night.

I have no appetite.
②

I feel dizzy sometimes.
③

I feel palpitations, too.
④

I've also been constipated for some time.
⑤

I think that is why

I have hemorrhoids.
⑥

Oh dear, that doesn't sound good...
⑦　　　　　　　　　　　⑧

---

⑤ constipate　を便秘させる
⑥ hemorrhoids　痔（複数扱い）
⑦ Oh dear.　まあまあ、どうしましょう
⑧ sound A　Aのように思われる

病院③

ベッドに仰向けに寝てください

ここは痛みますか？

はい、鈍い痛みがあります

ここはどうですか？

痛い！

刺すような痛みです

血圧を測りましょう

随分と血圧が高いですね

血液検査もしましょう

英語表現
① on one's back　仰向けに
② hurt　痛む
③ dull　形 鈍い
④ blood pressure　血圧

At the Doctor 3

Lie down on the bed on your back, please.
①

Does this hurt?
②

Yes. I have a dull pain there.
③

How's this?

アウチ
Ouch!

A sharp pain.

Let's take your blood pressure.
④

オーフリィ
It's awfully high.
⑤

We should have your blood tested, too.

⑤ awfully　副 ものすごく

病院④

どうでしたか、検査の結果は？

血糖値が異常に高いですね

糖尿病です

入院しなければなりませんか？

その必要はありません

しかし、当分通院が必要です

食事も制限しなければなりません

酒・タバコは止めてください

薬を処方します

英語表現

① blood sugar level　血糖値
② unusually　圖 異常に
③ diagnose　を診断する
④ diabetic　糖尿病患者

At the Doctor 4

How do the results of my test look?

Your blood sugar level's unusually high.
① ②

You're diagnosed as a diabetic.
③ ④

Do I have to be hospitalized?
⑤

That's not necessary.

But you need to see a doctor regularly for a while.
⑥

You also have to restrict your diet.
⑦

No drinking or smoking, either.

I'll write a prescription for your medication.
⑧ ⑨

⑤ be hospitalized　入院する
⑥ regularly　副 定期的に
⑦ restrict　を制限する
⑧ prescription　処方箋　　　　　　⑨ medication　医薬

163

ドライブ

ねえっ、ドライブに行かない？

本当に？　いいわよ

でも、ちゃんと安全運転してね

ドライブの前にガソリン満タンにしなくっちゃ

あれ、エンジンがかからない

どうしたんだろう？

バッテリー、上がっちゃったよ

それからタイヤもパンクしてる

やれやれ…

英語表現
① fill up A　A をいっぱいに満たす
② How come...?　どうして？（Why...? より口語的）
③ What's wrong?　どうしたの？
④ dead　形（電池などが）切れている

Going for a Drive

Hey, do you want to go for a drive with me?

Really? Why not?

But promise me to drive safely.

I have to <u>fill it up</u> with gas before we go.
　　　　　①

<u>How come</u> the engine's not running?
②

<u>What's wrong</u> with it?
③

The battery's <u>dead</u>.
　　　　　④

Tires are <u>flat</u>, too.
　　　　⑤

<u>Oh boy</u>...
⑥

⑤ flat 形 空気の抜けた
⑥ Oh boy. おや、まあ（驚きや喜びを表す）

165

自動車事故

キキキ～ッ、ドカーン！！

ああ、なんてこった！

大丈夫ですか？

ケガはありませんか？

あなたが突然出てくるから悪いんです

あなたが標識を無視したんでしょ

いずれにしても警察を呼びましょう

もしもし、事故を起こしました

怪我人がいます

英語表現

① screech　キーッと音を立てる（本文は擬音のため ch は省略）
② bang　ドーンという音
③ hurt　に怪我をさせる
④ rush out　突進して出てくる

Car Accident

Screeeee, bang!!
スクリ〜 バング
① ②

Oh, Jesus!

Are you all right?

Are you hurt?
③

It's your fault, suddenly rushing out into the street like that.
④

You ignored the sign!
イグノー(ァ)ド
⑤ ⑥

In either case, let's call the police.
⑦

Hello, there's been a car accident.
⑧

We have an injured person here.
⑨

⑤ignore を無視する
⑥sign 標識
⑦in either case どちらの場合でも
⑧there's been (=there has been)
⑨injured 形 怪我をした

167

犯罪①

おい、動くな！

何をするんですか？

失礼ですね

手を離して！

大声を出しますよ

これが見えないか

へたな真似をすると殺すぞ

どうか撃たないで！

金目の物を全部出せ！

英語表現

① get one's hands off A　Aから手を離す
② scream　悲鳴を上げる
③ stupid　形 ばかな
④ shoot　を撃つ

Crime 1

Don't move!

What are you doing?

Excuse me.

Get your hands off me!
①

I'll scream.
②
スクリーム

Look at this. Can't you see?

I'll kill you if you do anything stupid.
③
ステューピド

Don't shoot me!
④

Give me all your valuables!
⑤
ヴァリュ(ア)ブルズ

⑤ valuables （ふつう複数形で）貴重品

犯罪②

誰か助けて〜！

泥棒です！

彼を捕まえて！

あいつです！

向こうへ逃げてる男です

どうしたんですか？

男に襲われました

私のバッグを奪っていきました

中に現金が10万円入っています

英語表現

① robbery　盗難
② get done　…される
③ rob　を奪う
④ take　を奪う

Crime 2

Somebody, help me!

Robbery!
①
ラ バ リィ

Catch him!

That's him!

The guy running away over there.

What happened?

I got robbed by a man.
② ③
ラ ブ ド

He took my bag.
④

I had 100,000 yen in cash in there.

第 5 章

そろそろ日も沈むころ、英語だけですごせた？

頼みごと

いま手は空いていますか？

実は頼みたいことがあるんですが…

なんでしょう？

自分にできることでしたらいいですよ

そう言っていただけると助かります

この家具を動かしたいのです

なんだ、そんなことですか

お安いご用です

他に何かできることはありませんか？

英語表現

① give...a hand　…に手を貸す
② I would like to ask you a favor.／May I ask a favor of you?　お願いがあるのですが
③ appreciate　をありがたく思う

Asking a Favor

Can you give me a hand?
①

Actually, I would like to ask you a favor...
②

What is it?

I'll help if it's something I can do.

I appreciate your offer.
③   ④

I want to move this furniture.
ファ～ニチャ

That's not too hard.
⑤

A piece of cake.
⑥

Anything else that I can do for you?

④ offer　申し出
⑤ hard　形 困難な
⑥ a piece of cake　楽な仕事、朝飯前のこと

デートに誘う①

綾子さん、今日の夕方何か予定ある？

どうして？

今夜夕食をいっしょにどうですか？

ごめんなさい、今日は用事があるの

8時までに家に帰らないといけないの

でもお茶ぐらいならいいわよ

それでもかまいません

私は6時に会社の前で待ってます

それでは後ほど…

英語表現
① have dinner　食事をする
② have plans　計画がある
③ get home　帰宅する
④ by　…までには

Asking Someone for a Date 1

Ayako, do you have plans this evening?

Why do you ask?

Would you like to <u>have dinner</u> with me?
①

I'm sorry, but I <u>have plans</u> today.
②

I have to <u>get home</u> <u>by</u> 8.
③ ④

But I have time for some tea.

That'll be great.

Then, I'll see you in front of the office at 6.

<u>Catch you later</u>...
⑤

⑤ Catch you later.　あとでね

デートに誘う②

裕子さん、今週の週末は暇？

ええ、暇よ

いっしょに映画でも見に行きませんか？

ええ、よろこんで

ちょうど映画に行きたかったところなのよ

どこで待ち合わせしましょう？

渋谷の109の前はどう？

ええ、そこにしましょう

ところで何時に待ち合わせします？

英語表現

① free 形 暇な
② I'd（＝I would）
③ I'd be happy to. よろこんで
④ Shall we...? …しましょうか？

Asking Someone for a Date 2

Yuko, are you <u>free</u> this weekend?
①

Yeah, I'm free.

Would you like to go to a movie with me?

Sure, <u>I'd be happy to.</u>
②③

I was just thinking of going to a movie, too.

Where <u>shall we</u> meet?
④

<u>Maybe</u>, in front of the 109 in Shibuya?
⑤

Sure, that'll be fine.

By the way, what time should we meet?

⑤ **maybe** （提案）…しましょうか

デートに誘う③

幸子さん、この間のデートの件だけど…

来週の日曜日どうですか？

ごめんなさい、やっぱりダメです

予定が入ってしまったの

じゃ、8日の休日はどう？

その日もダメです

じゃ、いつがいいんですか？

ここのところ忙しくて暇がないの

また別の機会にお願いできる？

英語表現
① the other day　先日
② make it　都合をつける
③ on　（特定の日などをあらわして）…に
④ pretty　副 かなり

Asking Someone for a Date 3

Sachiko, about the date we were talking about the other day...
①

Is next Sunday OK for you?

I'm sorry I can't make it.
②

I have an appointment.

Well, what about the 8th, on the national holiday?

I can't go on that day, either.
③

Then, when is good for you?

I've been pretty busy these days.
④ ⑤

Can you ask me again some other time?
⑥

⑤ these days　このごろ
⑥ time　機会

アフター6

もう外は暗くなってきたね

そろそろ仕事を終わりにしない？

ああ、そうしよう

俺はまだ仕事が終わらないんだ

今日は残業するのかい？

ああ、そうなりそうだね

今日は給料日だし

いっしょに飲みに行こうよ

なんなら俺、手伝うよ

英語表現

① get dark　暗くなる
② wrap up　（仕事などを）終える
③ should　…したほうがいい
④ work overtime　残業する

182

After Work

It's getting dark outside.
①

Should we start wrapping up?
②

Yeah, we should.
③

I can't finish my work, yet.

Are you working overtime today?
④

Looks like it.
⑤

It's payday today, so
⑥

let's go out for a drink together.

I can help you if you want.

⑤ looks like A　A になりそうである
⑥ payday　給料日

夕方

ただいま

おかえりなさい

あなた、今日は早かったわね

何かあったの？

いや別に…

それにしても疲れた

へとへとだ

食事はまだかい？

まだ用意できてないわよ

英語表現

① Hi, honey.　「おかえり」というフレーズは英語にはない
② (I've got) nothing special.　とくに何もない
③ exhaust　を疲れ果てさせる
④ ready　圏 用意ができた

Evening

I'm home.

Hi, honey.
①

You're early today.

Did something happen?

Nothing special...
②

Oh boy, I'm tired.

イグゾーステド
I'm exhausted.
③

Isn't it dinnertime, yet?

Dinner's not ready, yet.
④

夕食①

ママ、今日のご飯は何？

今日はカレーよ

もう食べられる？

あと30分ほど待って

さあ、できた

夕食の時間よ

やっとだね

いま行くよ

ちゃんと手を洗った？

英語表現

① What's for dinner?　ご飯は何？
② A or so　Aかそこら
③ right 副 すぐに
④ good（＝well）副 よく（米話）

Dinner 1

Mom, what's for dinner tonight?
①

Curry.

Can we eat now?

Wait for another 30 minutes or so.
②

Dinner's ready.

It's time to eat.

Finally.

Be right there.
③

Did you wash your hands good?
④

夕食②

わぁ〜、おいしそう

いいにおい

もう腹ぺこだよ

いただきます

召し上がれ

おかわりはある？

心配しなくてもあるわよ

ごちそうさま

もうおなか一杯だ

英語表現

① good 形 おいしい
② smell A Aのにおいがする
③ I'm starving.（＝I'm starved.） おなかがペコペコだ
④ starve 腹ぺこである

Dinner 2

Wow, it looks good.
①

Smells good.
②

I'm starving.
③ ④
(スターヴィング)

Let's eat.
⑤

Enjoy your dinner.

Is there enough for another serving?

Don't worry. There's plenty.
⑥

Good dinner, Mom.
⑦

God, I'm so full.

⑤ Let's eat.　「いただきます」のフレーズに相当する英語はない
⑥ plenty　副 たっぷり
⑦ Good dinner, Mom.　「ごちそうさま」のフレーズに相当する
　　　　　　　　　　英語はない

189

お出かけ

おい、お前、用意はできたかい？

まだよ

もう少し待って

パーティーに遅れるじゃないか

さっきからもう30分も待ってるんだよ

そうせかさないで

女は色々と大変なのよ

そんな言い訳はいいから

早くしてくれよ

英語表現

① ready　形 用意ができている
② for　…の間
③ rush　を急がせる
④ excuse　言い訳

Going Out

Hey, honey, are you ready?
①

Not yet.

Give me a few more minutes.

We'll be late for the party.

I've been waiting for you for more than half
②
an hour.

Don't rush me.
③

Women have many things to do.

Don't give me such an excuse.
④

Just hurry up.
⑤

⑤ hurry up　急ぐ（主に命令文で用いる）

レストラン①

いらっしゃいませ

何名様ですか？

2名です

できれば窓際がいいんですが

かしこまりました

こちらにどうぞ

メニューです

お決まりになりましたらお呼びください

わかりました

英語表現

① by 　…のそばの
② Certainly. 　（返事に用いて）承知しました
③ this way 　（副詞的に用いて）こちらの方向へ
④ decide 　決める

Restaurant 1

Can I help you?

How many?

Two, please.

Could we get a table by the window?
①

Certainly.
②

Come this way, please.
③

Here's your menu.

Let me know when you've decided.
④

We will.

レストラン②

もうお決まりになりましたか？

注文してよろしいですか？

ええ、お願いします

ところで、お薦めは何かありますか？

色々とございますが…

今日のお薦めは何ですか？

チキンのトマト煮でございます

じゃ、それをもらおうか

それから、これはどんな料理？

英語表現

① yet 副（疑問文で）もう
② go ahead さあ、どうぞ
③ special 特別サービス料理
④ dish 料理

Restaurant 2

Have you decided, yet?
①

Can we order now?

Sure go ahead.
②

By the way, do you have any specials?
③

We have a few specials...

What is today's special?

That'll be chicken tomato stew.

Well, I'll take that, please.

And, what kind of dish is this?
④

レストラン③

ええっと、これとこれをください

そして大根サラダももらおうか

私も同じものいただけますか

他に何か注文はありませんか？

そんなところかな…

肉の具合はいかがいたしますか？

よく焼いてください

飲み物はいかがなさいますか？

赤ワインのグラスを2つお願いします

英語表現
① um　うむ、えーっと（ためらいの声）
② radish　ハツカダイコン
③ the same　同じもの
④ anything else　何かほかのもの

Restaurant 3

<u>Umm</u>, can I get this and this?
①

And also a <u>radish</u> salad.
②
ラ ディ シ

I'll have <u>the same</u>, please.
③

<u>Anything else</u> for you?
④

<u>That's it</u>...
⑤

How would you like your meat done?

Well-done, please.

Something to drink?

Two glasses of red wine, please.

⑤ That's it.　それでおしまい

197

レストラン④

遅いな〜…

注文した料理がまだ来ないよ

君、まだ料理が来ないが…

いったいどうなってるんだ？

すみません、もうじきまいります

あとどのくらいかかるんだ？

もう20分も待たされているんだよ

恐れ入ります、もうしばらくお待ちください

あっ、来た来た

英語表現
① so 副 とても
② dinner 食事
③ serve （飲食物）を出す
④ nearly 副 ほぼ

Restaurant 4

So slow...
①

Our dinner's not here, yet.
②

Excuse me, our dinner's not here...

What is going on?

I'm sorry. They'll be served soon.
③

How many more minutes will it take?

We've been waiting for nearly 20 minutes.
④

ペイシェンス
I'm very sorry. I appreciate your patience.
⑤   ⑥

Oh, here they come.
⑦

⑤ appreciate をありがたく思う
⑥ patience 忍耐
⑦ here （文頭で）ほら

199

レストラン⑤

料理が冷めてしまうよ

先に食べて

どう、おいしい？

ウェ〜ッ！

何、これ？

これ、変な味がする

どんな味？

なんだか腐った味がするけど

どれどれ…

英語表現

① get A　しだいに A になる
② yuck　おえっ、ゲッ
③ It's got（＝It has got、＝it has）
④ have got　を持っている

Restaurant 5

Dinner's going to get cold.
①

Go ahead and eat.

How is it?

Yuck!
ヤック
②

What is this?

It's got a strange taste.
③ ④

What does it taste like?

It tastes kind of like something rotten.
⑤ ⑥ ラトゥン ⑦

Let me taste it...

⑤ taste like A　Aのような味がする
⑥ kind of　いくらか
⑦ rotten　形 腐った

レストラン⑥

どう料理の味は？

そんなに悪くないよ

まあまあだね

これ食べられる？

それは食べられないよ

この肉、堅いわ

これは味が濃い

これは油っこい

これはすごく辛い

英語表現

① acceptable 形 受け入れられる
② worth doing …するだけの価値がある
③ tough 形 （肉などが）堅い
④ season （食べ物）に味つけする

Restaurant 6

How's the food?

Not bad.

It's acceptable.
①
アクセプタブル

Is this worth eating?
②
ワ～ス

No, it's not worth eating.

This meat is tough.
③

This is seasoned too much.
④
スィーズンド

This is so greasy.
⑤
グリースィ

This is really hot.

⑤ greasy 形 油っこい

レストラン⑦

料理はいかがですか？

こんなおいしい料理、生まれて初めてです

それはよかった

でも、もうおなかいっぱい

もう入りません

ちょっと食べ過ぎてしまったみたいです

もう1杯ワインはいかがですか？

もうけっこうです

充分にいただきました

英語表現

① How do you like A?　A はいかがですか？
② in one's life　生まれてからいままでに
③ be stuffed　おなかがいっぱいである
④ not...anymore　もうこれ以上は…ない

204

Restaurant 7

How do you like the food?
①

I've never had such a delicious dish in my life before.
②

I'm glad you like it.

スタッフト
But I'm so stuffed,
③

and I can't eat anymore.
④

I think I ate too much.

Would you like another glass of wine?

No, thank you.

I had enough.

支払い

お勘定をお願いします

どこで支払えばいいですか？

向こうのレジでお願いします

ここは私にご馳走させてください

いえ、割り勘にしましょう

支払いは別々でお願いします

私の分はおいくら？

私が誘ったのですから…

私に支払わせてください

英語表現
① check　（レストランなどの）伝票
② register　レジ
③ take care of A　Ａの世話をする
④ split　を分ける

206

Payment

Can I have the <u>check</u>, please?
①

Where should I pay?

At the <u>register</u> over there, please.
②　　レヂスタァ

Let me <u>take care of</u> the check tonight.
③

No, let's <u>split</u> it.
④　スプリット

Can we pay <u>separately</u>, please?
⑤　　　セパレトリィ

How much is it for me?

I <u>invited</u> you...
⑥

So let me pay the bill.

⑤ separately 副 別々に
⑥ invite を招待する

映画

何の映画が見たい？

そうねえ、いまスピルバーグの映画やってるよね

それが見たいな

どこの映画館で上映しているのかな

とりあえず近くの映画館に行ってみよう

ねえ、ここでやってるよ

すみません、次の上映は何時からですか？

8時から上映です

上映が終了する時間は何時ですか？

英語表現
① run （映画が）続映される
② just 副 ちょっと
③ show を上映する
④ end 終わる

Movie

Which movie do you want to see?

Let me think. Spielberg movie is <u>running</u> now, isn't it?
①

I want to see that.

I wonder which theater it's in.

Let's <u>just</u> first go to the nearest theater.
②

Oh yeah. They're <u>showing</u> it here.
③

Excuse me. What time is the next show?

The next one's at 8.

What time will the movie <u>end</u>?
④

カラオケ

ねえ、カラオケに行かない？

僕はあまり歌が得意じゃないんだけれど…

そんなこと言わないで行こうよ

わかった、付き合うよ

君が先に歌って

うまい、うまい

君は歌が上手だね

次はあなたの番よ

何を歌うの？

英語表現

① actually 圖 実際には
② be good at A Aがじょうずである
③ go with A Aといっしょに行く
④ first 圖 最初に

Karaoke

Hey, do you want to go to Karaoke?

Actually, I'm not very good at singing...
①   ②

Don't say that. Let's go.

OK. I'll go with you.
③

You sing first.
④

Very good.

You sing well.

You're next.
⑤

What are you going to sing?
⑥

⑤ next 形 次の
⑥ be going to do …するつもりだ

211

愛の告白

君に話があるんだ

何よ、そんなに改まって？

君はいま誰か好きな男性がいるかい？

いいえ、いまは誰もいないわ

それはよかった

僕のことどう思う？

とても素敵よ

僕は君に一目ぼれしてしまったんだ

できたら僕と付き合ってくれないか？

英語表現
① serious 形 まじめな
② be in love with A A に恋してる
③ think of A A のことを考える
④ fall in love with A A に恋する

Confessing Love to Someone

I need to talk to you.

What is it? Why so serious?
①

Are you in love with someone right now?
②

No. There's nobody now.

That's good.

What do you think of me?
③

You're a nice person.

I fell in love with you the first time I saw you.
④

Can we start seeing each other, if it's OK
with you?
⑤

⑤ see　と交際する

テレビ

テレビでも見ようか？

何か面白いものやってる？

テレビつけてみて

7チャンネルは何をやってるかな？

この番組はつまらないわ

他に何かやってない？

チャンネルを変えて

野球は8時からだっけ？

私、野球はいやよ！

英語表現

① Shall we...?　…しましょうか？
② interesting　圏 おもしろい
③ on　圓 行われて
④ turn on　（テレビなど）をつける

TV

Shall we watch some TV?
①

Is something interesting on?
②　③

Turn on the TV.
④

What is on Channel 7 right now?

This show is boring.
⑤　　　ボー(ァ)リング
　　　　　⑥

Is anything else on?

Change the channel.

Baseball is on at 8, isn't it?

I don't want to watch baseball!

⑤ show　番組
⑥ boring　形 退屈な

飲み屋①

この店にしよう

ここにはよく来るの？

そんなに来ないけど…

わあっ、人が一杯だ

空いている席あるかな…？

あそこに席が空いているよ

そこにしよう

今日は飲むぞ〜！

仕事のことは忘れて楽しもう

英語表現

① that　副 そんなに
② crowded　形 込み合った
③ left　leave の過去分詞
④ take　（いす）に座る

216

Bar 1

Let's go to this bar.

Do you come here often?

Not that often...
①

Wow! So crowded.
②

Are there any seats left?
③

There're some seats.

Let's take those.
④

I'm going to drink tonight!

Let's forget about work and have fun.
⑤

⑤ have fun 楽しむ

飲み屋②

何飲む？

まずはビールで乾杯しよう

ビンと生どっちにする？

生ビールがいいな

それでは乾杯！

さあ、ぐぐっと一気に飲もう！

うまい！

今日は僕のおごりだ

遠慮せずに飲んでくれ

英語表現

① give a toast　乾杯する
② draft beer　生ビール
③ prefer　のほうを好む
④ Cheers!　乾杯！

Bar 2

What are we having?

Let's give a toast with beer first.
①

Bottle or draft?
　　　　ドゥラフト
②

I prefer draft.
③

Well then, cheers!
　　　　チアーズ
④

Come on!　Drink up!
⑤

This is so good!

It's on me tonight.
⑥

Go ahead and drink a lot.

⑤ Come on!　（相手をうながして）さあ！
⑥ It's on me.　私のおごりです

飲み屋③

君は酒が強いね

まだ飲むつもりなの？

よくそんなに飲めるもんだな

僕は酒に弱いから

もう酔っちゃったよ

本当に飲み過ぎちゃった

こんなに飲むんじゃなかった

なんだか気持ちが悪くなってきたよ

トイレはどこにある？

英語表現

① quite 副 かなり
② handle を取り扱う
③ drinking 飲酒
④ drunk 形 酒に酔った

Bar 3

You can drink <u>quite</u> a lot, can't you?
①

Are you going to drink more?

I don't know how you can drink like that.

I can't <u>handle</u> <u>drinking</u>, so
②   ③

I'm already <u>drunk</u>.
ドゥランク
④

I actually had too much drink.

I <u>shouldn't have drunk</u> this much.
⑤

I'm feeling kind of sick.

Where is the bathroom?

⑤ shouldn't have done …すべきでなかった

夜のひととき

ねえ、久美子、お風呂先に入っていいかい？

どうぞお先に

お湯加減はどう？

ちょうどいいよ！

ああ、気持ちがいい

いっぺんに疲れが取れるよ

お前も入らないかい？

もうちょっと待って

すぐに行くから…

英語表現

① take a bath　風呂に入る
② tub　湯ぶね
③ perfect　形 申し分のない
④ relaxing　形 こころ休まるような

At Night

Hey, Kumiko, can I take a bath before you?
①

Sure, go ahead.

How's the tub?
②

It's perfect!
③

Ah, it feels so good.

This is so relaxing.
④

Why don't you get in, too?

Just a second.
⑤

I'll be right there...

⑤ second　ちょっとの間

就寝

ふあ～っ

あくびが出ちゃった

眠いと思ったらもう12時だ

もう寝る時間ね

明日の朝は早いし

早く寝ましょう

目覚まし、合わせた?

ああ、ちゃんとセットしたよ

あなた、おやすみなさい

英語表現

① can't help doing …せずにはいられない
② yawn あくびをする
③ No wonder... …は不思議ではない
④ bedtime 就寝時間

Going to Bed

Ｙaaaawn...
ヨ ～ ン

I can't help yawning...
①   ②

It's midnight. No wonder I'm sleepy.
                ③

It's already bedtime, eh?
                ④

We have to get up early tomorrow, so

let's go to bed now.
       ⑤

Did you set the alarm?

Yeah. I did.

Good night, honey.

⑤ go to bed   寝る

225

ヤバいくらい使える
「起きてから寝るまで」英会話

著　者　　リック西尾
発行者　　真船美保子
発行所　　KK ロングセラーズ
　　　　　東京都新宿区高田馬場 2-1-2　〒 169-0075
　　　　　電話（03）3204-5161（代）　振替 00120-7-145737
　　　　　http://www.kklong.co.jp
印　刷　　中央精版印刷(株)　製　本　(株)難波製本

落丁・乱丁はお取り替えいたします。
※定価と発行日はカバーに表示してあります。
ISBN978-4-8454-5056-5　C0282　　Printed In Japan 2018